Computation Theory Lecture Note

Taeho Jo

 Alpha AI Publication

Computation Theory: Lecture Note

Copyright © 2024 Alpha AI Publication

All rights reserved by publisher, Alpha AI Publication. No part of this publication may be reproduced or transmitted in any form by any means, electronic, mechanical, photocopying, recording, or otherwise without prior written permission of the publisher.

About Author, Taeho Jo, President of Alpha AI Publication

The author of this book, Taeho Jo, is the founder of the publishing company, Alpha AI Publication, to which the copyright of this book belongs. His specialty is artificial intelligence; he got his Bachelor from Korea University, his Master from POSTECH (Pohang University of Science and Technology), and PhD from University of Ottawa. He has careers in both industrial organizations, Samsung SDS, ETRI (Electronic and Telecommunication Research Institute), and KISTI (Korea Institute of Science and Technology Information) and academic organizations, Inha University and Hongik University as a professor. He has published more than 200 research papers in journals and proceedings, and three books on text mining, machine learning, and deep learning under the contract with the publishing company, Springer, and awarded three times in Marquis Who's Who in the World. The author of this book, Taeho Jo, has a very strong vision for the future as a pioneer of artificial intelligence.

Computation Theory

Lecturer: Taeho Jo

Contents

- Lecture 1 Introduction---------------------------------------3
- Lecture 2 Finite State Automata-----------------------------30
- Lecture 3 Regular Expression--------------------------------57
- Lecture 4 Regular Languages Properties---------------------84
- Lecture 5 Context Free Languages---------------------------111
- Lecture 6 Context Free Grammar Simplification-----------138
- Lecture 7 Pushdown Automata-----------------------------165
- Lecture 8 Context Free Languages Properties-------------192

Introduction

Lecture 01

Outline

- Overview of Computation Theory
- Review of Discrete Mathematics
- Proof Techniques
- Language and Grammar
- Summary and Exercise

Overview of Computation Theory

- Definition of Automata
    - Mathematical and Abstract Model of Hardware Computer
    - Accept an Input as a String and Generate "Accept" or "Reject" as its Output (Binary Output)
    - Definition of Formal Language as set of Strings which is accepted
    - Abstraction of Programming Languages

Overview of Computation Theory

- Automata Visualization

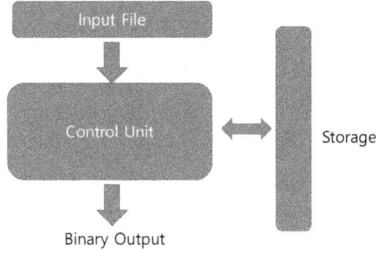

Overview of Computation Theory

- Transition Function
    - Definition of States
    - Input: Current State and a Character
    - Output: Next State
    - Transition from one State to next State by a String

Overview of Computation Theory

- Output of Automata
  - Binary Output
    - Yes as Accept the Input String
    - No as Reject the Input String
  - Check for the Correct or Incorrect Syntax
  - Starting in the Initial State
  - If it researches the Final State by Transition Function, it accepts the Input String
  - Otherwise, it rejects it

Overview of Computation Theory

- Goal of this Lecture
  - Establish the Background by Reviewing Discrete Mathematics
  - Obtain the Two Proof Techniques: Induction and Contradiction
  - Understand the Concepts of Language and Grammar
  - Obtain the Ability to check whether a string is grammatically correct or not

Review of Discrete Mathematics

- List of Topics
    - Sets
    - Function and Relation
    - Equivalence
    - Graphs and Trees

Review of Discrete Mathematics

- Sets
  - Set: A Collection of Items by Membership
  - Set Operations: Intersection, Union, and Difference
  - Universal Set, Subset, Complementation, and Empty Set
  - Power Set and Cartesian Product

Review of Discrete Mathematics

- Functions and Relations
    - Function as Rule of Assigning an Element of a particular set to an Element of the Other Set
    - Input Set as the Domain and Output Set as the Range
    - Single Element of Output Set (Range) mapped by an Element of Input Set → Function
    - Multiple Elements of Output Set (Range) mapped by One → Relation

Review of Discrete Mathematics

- Equivalence
    - Equivalence Relation between x and y →   Keep the Three Rules
    - Reflexive Rule:
    - Symmetry Rule: $\forall x, x \equiv x$
    - Transitive Rule:
    $$\forall x, y, x \equiv y \rightarrow y \equiv x$$
    $$\forall x, y, z, (x \equiv y) \wedge (y \equiv z) \rightarrow x \equiv z$$

Review of Discrete Mathematics

- Graphs and Trees
  - Graph: Consists of Two Sets: Vertex Set and Edge Set
  - Vertex Set: $V = \{v_1, v_2, \ldots, v_n\}$
  - Each Edge as a Pair of Vertices: $e_i = (v_j, v_k)$
  - Tree as a Directed Graph
    - No Cycle
    - Start from a Single Vertex (Node) called Root Node
    - Edge $e_i = (v_j, v_k)$: v_j → Parent Node and v_k → Childe Node
    - #Paths from Root Node to Current Node → Level

Proof Techniques

- Proof by Induction
    - Infer Truth of the Current Statement from Examples
    - Basis: Proving Truth from its Basic Example
    - Induction Assumption: Assuming the Current Statement is True
    - Induction Step: Proving it by Extending the Current Statement

Proof Techniques

- Summation
  - Prove $\sum_{k=1}^{n} k = \dfrac{n(n+1)}{2}$
  - Basis: $\sum_{k=1}^{0} k = 0$, $\sum_{k=1}^{1} k = 1$, $\sum_{k=1}^{2} k = 3$
  - Induction Assumption: $\sum_{k=1}^{n} k = \dfrac{n(n+1)}{2}$
  - Induction Step

$$\sum_{k=1}^{n+1} k = \sum_{k=1}^{n} k + (n+1) = \dfrac{n(n+1)}{2} + (n+1)$$
$$= \dfrac{(n+1)(n+2)}{2}$$

Proof Techniques

- Summation of Square
  - Prove $\sum_{k=1}^{n} k^2 = \frac{n(n+1)(2n+1)}{6}$
  - Basis: $\sum_{k=1}^{0} k^2 = 0$, $\sum_{k=1}^{1} k^2 = 1$, $\sum_{k=1}^{2} k^2 = 5$
  - Induction Assumption: $\sum_{k=1}^{n} k^2 = \frac{n(n+1)(2n+1)}{6}$
  - Induction Step

$$\sum_{k=1}^{n+1} k^2 = \frac{n(n+1)(2n+1)}{6} + (n+1)^2 = \frac{(n+1)(n+2)(2n+3)}{6}$$

Proof Techniques

- Binary Tree
  - Prove the binary tree with its height, n, has at most 2^n leaves
  - Basis: $l(n) \leq 2^n$
  - Induction Assumption: $l(0) \leq 1, l(1) \leq 2, l(2) \leq 4$ True
  - Induction Step

$$l(n) \leq 2^n$$

$$l(n+1) = 2l(n) \leq 2 \cdot 2^n = 2^{n+1}$$

Proof Techniques

- Proof by Contradiction
  - Prove $\sqrt{2}$ is an irrational number
  - Assume that $\sqrt{2}$ is a rational number

$$\sqrt{2} = \frac{m}{n} \rightarrow \text{Irreducible Fraction}$$

$$\sqrt{2} = \frac{m}{n} \quad\Longrightarrow\quad \begin{array}{l} m = 2k \\ 2n^2 = 4k^2 \\ n^2 = 2k^2 \end{array}$$

$$\sqrt{2}n = m,\ 2n^2 = m^2$$

  - Contradict with $\sqrt{2}$ is a rational number
  - $\sqrt{2}$ is an Irrational Number

Language and Grammar

- Overview of Language
  - Set of Acceptable Strings
  - Alphabet as an Atomic Character composed of a String
  - String as a Combination of Alphabets by Grammar
  - Subset of All Strings composing Alphabets

Language and Grammar

- Formal Definition of Language
  - Alphabet: $\Sigma = \{a, b\}$
  - Language as a Subset of $\Sigma^* = \{\lambda, a, b, ab, aa, ba, bb, ...\}$
  - Definition of Language $\Sigma^+ = \Sigma^* - \{\lambda\}$

$$L = \{a^n b^n : n \geq 0\}$$

Language and Grammar

- Operations on String
  - Each String → u, v, w
  - Concatenation
    $$w = a_1a_2,...,a_n$$
    $$v = b_1b_2,...,b_m$$
  - Reverse $\quad wv = a_1a_2,...,a_nb_1b_2,...,b_m$

    $$w = a_1a_2,...,a_n$$
    $$w^R = a_n...a_2a_1$$
  - Substring: Part of String

Language and Grammar

- Grammar
  - Rule for building a String which belong to the Language by combing Alphabets
  - Formal Definition:
  - Example

$$G = \{V, T, S, P\}$$
$$G = (\{S\}, \{a, b\}, S, P)$$

  - Derivation

$$S \rightarrow aSb, S \rightarrow \lambda$$

aabb

$S \Rightarrow aSb \Rightarrow aaSbb \Rightarrow aabb$

$S \stackrel{*}{\Rightarrow} aabb$

Language and Grammar

- Application to Programming Language
  - Variable in Java
  - Grammar:
  - Rules

  $G = (\{\langle id \rangle, \langle rest \rangle, \langle letter \rangle, \langle digit \rangle\}, \{a,..., z, 0,..., 9\}, \langle id \rangle, P)$

  $\langle id \rangle \to \langle letter \rangle \langle rest \rangle$
  $\langle rest \rangle \to \langle letter \rangle \langle rest \rangle \mid \langle digit \rangle \langle rest \rangle \mid \lambda$
  $\langle letter \rangle \to a \mid b \mid .... \mid z$

  - String

  $\langle digit \rangle \to 0 \mid 1 \mid .... \mid 9$

  $\langle id \rangle \stackrel{*}{\Rightarrow} a0$

Summary and Exercises

- Summary
    - Automata as Mathematical Model of Computer consisting of Input, Output, Temporary Storage, and Computation
    - Review of Discrete Mathematics as Back Ground: Sets, Function, Relation, and Graphs
    - Proof by Induction: Basis, Inductive Assumption, and Inductive Proof
    - Definition of Language, Grammar and their Relation

Summary and Exercises

- Function, Relation, and Equivalance
  - Function? $\{(1,5),(3,3),(1,2),(7,2)\}$
  - Function? $\{(1,5),(3,3),(5,2),(1,2)\}$
  - Show the equivalence of $x \approx y$
  - Show the equivalence of $x \bmod n = y \bmod n$

Summary and Exercises

- Proof by Induction in Sequence Summations
    - (1) $\sum_{k=1}^{n} a = na$
    - (2) $\sum_{k=1}^{n} 2k = n(n+1)$
    - (3) $2^n < n!$ for $n > 4$
    - Prove $\sqrt{3}$ is an irrational number

Summary and Exercises

- Grammar → Language

$G = (\{S\}, \{a,b\}, S, P)$
$P: S \to ab, S \to \lambda$

$G = (\{S\}, \{a,b\}, S, P)$
$P: S \to aS, S \to \lambda$

$G = (\{S\}, \{a,b\}, S, P)$
$P: S \to aSb, S \to \lambda$

$G = (\{S\}, \{a,b\}, S, P)$
$P: S \to aAb, A \to aSb, A \to \lambda$

Summary and Exercises

- Language → Grammar

$$L = \{a^n b^n : n = 1\}$$
$$L = \{a^n b^n : n \geq 0\}$$
$$L = \{a^n b^n : n \geq 1\}$$
$$L = \{a^m b^n : m \geq 1, n \geq 1\}$$

Finite State Automata

Lecture 02

Outline

- Introduction
- Deterministic State Automata
- Nondeterministic State Automata
- NFA → DFA
- Summary and Exercises

Introduction

- Overview of Finite Automata

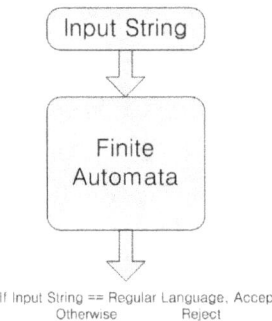

Introduction

- State Transition Graph 1

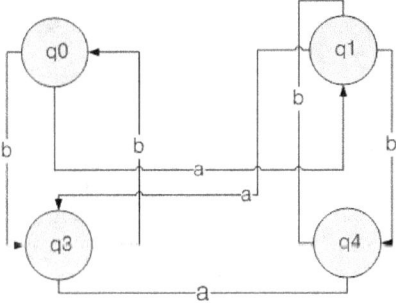

Introduction

- State Transition Graph 2

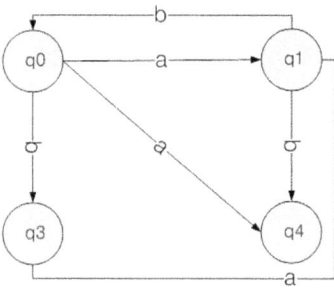

Introduction

- Conversion of State Transition Graph

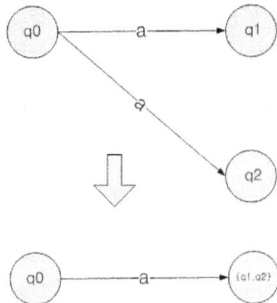

Introduction

- Goal of this Lecture
    - Model DFA into both Mathematical Notation and Transition Graph
    - Model DFA which accepts a particular pattern of string into them
    - Model NFA into both Mathematical Notation and Transition Graph
    - Convert NFA into its equivalent DFA

Deterministic State Automata

- Definition of DFA
    - Quintuple: $M = (Q, \Sigma, \delta, q_0, F)$
    - Q : State Set Σ : Alphabet Set
    - Transition Function: $\delta : Q \times \Sigma \to Q$
    - $\delta(q_0, a) = q_1$: (q0) —a→ (q1)
    - : Initial State   : Final State Set
    - $q_0 \in Q$ $F \subseteq Q$

Deterministic State Automata

- Transition Graph ←→ DFA

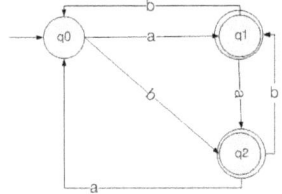

$M = (\{q_0, q_1, q_2\}, \{a, b\}, \delta, q_0, \{q_1, q_2\})$
$\delta(q_0, a) = q_1, \delta(q_0, b) = q_2$
$\delta(q_1, a) = q_2, \delta(q_1, b) = q_0$
$\delta(q_2, a) = q_0, \delta(q_2, b) = q_1$

Deterministic State Automata

- Language accepted by DFA
    - Language: $L(M) = \{w \in \Sigma^* : \delta^*(q_0, w) \in F\}$
    - Extended Transition Function

        $\delta^*(q, \lambda) = q$

        $\delta^*(q, wa) = \delta(\delta^*(q, w), a)$

- $\delta^*(q_i, w) = q_j$ if and only if there is a walk from the state q_i to the state q_j
- Trap State: State with no walk to a final state

Deterministic State Automata

- String with Prefix "aab"

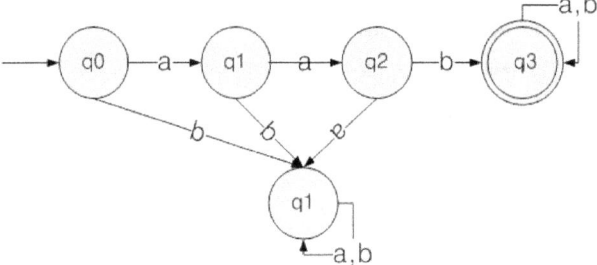

Deterministic State Automata

- Any String not including "aab"

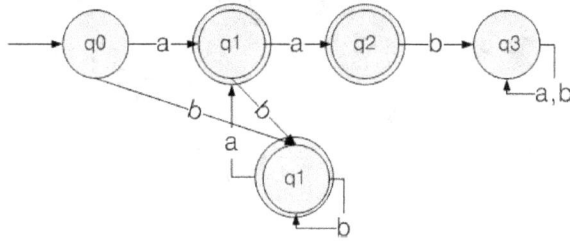

Nondeterministic State Automata

- Definition of NFA
  - Quintuple: $M = (Q, \Sigma, \delta, q_0, F)$
    - Q : State Set
    - Σ : Alphabet Set
  - Transition Function:
    $$\delta : Q \times (\Sigma \cup \{\lambda\}) \to 2^Q$$
    $$\delta(q_0, a) = \{q_1, q_2\}$$
    - $q_0 \in Q$: Initial State
    - $F \subseteq Q$: Final State Set

Nondeterministic State Automata

- Transition Graph ←→ NFA

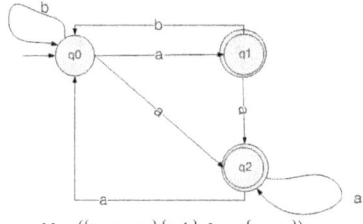

$M = (\{q_0, q_1, q_2\}, \{a, b\}, \delta, q_0, \{q_1, q_2\})$
$\delta(q_0, a) = \{q_1, q_2\}, \delta(q_0, b) = \{q_0\}$
$\delta(q_1, a) = \{q_2\}, \delta(q_1, b) = \{q_0\}$
$\delta(q_2, a) = \{q_0, q_2\}, \delta(q_2, b) = \varnothing$

Nondeterministic State Automata

- Language accepted by NFA

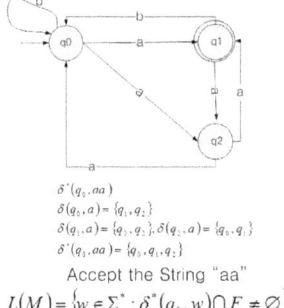

$\delta^*(q_0, aa)$
$\delta(q_0, a) = \{q_1, q_2\}$
$\delta(q_1, a) = \{q_2, q_2\}, \delta(q_2, a) = \{q_0, q_1\}$
$\delta^*(q_0, aa) = \{q_0, q_1, q_2\}$

Accept the String "aa"

$$L(M) = \{w \in \Sigma^* : \delta^*(q_0, w) \cap F \neq \varnothing\}$$

Nondeterministic State Automata

- Special Transitions in NFA

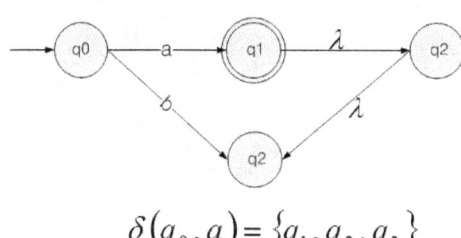

$$\delta(q_0, a) = \{q_1, q_2, q_3\}$$
$$\delta(q_2, a) = \varnothing$$

Nondeterministic State Automata

- DFA vs NFA

	DFA	NFA
Transition Function	Output: State	Output: State Set
Default Transition	Not Available	Available
Accept Condition	Reach a Final State	Existence of any Final State among Reachable States
Accepted Language		Regular Language

NFA → DFA

- Procedure of NFA → DFA
  - Create the Graph, G_D with the Initial State $\{q_0\}$
  - Do for all Edges $\{q_i, q_j, ..., q_k\}$
    - Take the Vertex of $\delta^*(q_i,a)$ $\delta^*(q_j,a)$ without Outgoing Edge
    - Compute $\{q_l, q_m, ..., q_n\}$ ... $\delta^*(q_i,a)$ $\delta^*(q_j,a)$ $\delta^*(q_k,a)$
    - Set: G_D by union of ..... $\{q_l, q_m, ..., q_n\}$
    - If it does not exist previously, add the vertex $\{q_l, q_m, ..., q_n\}$
    - Add the edge between $\{q_i, q_j, ..., q_k\}$ and $\{q_l, q_m, ..., q_n\}$ labeled with 'a'
  - Set every State whose label includes the final state
  - If NFA accepts the empty string, set the Initial state as a Final State

NFA → DFA

- NFA → DFA 1

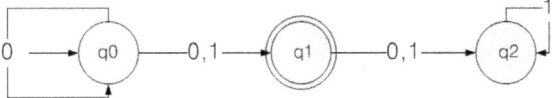

NFA → DFA

- NFA → DFA 2

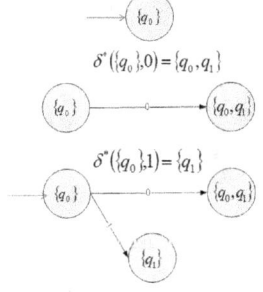

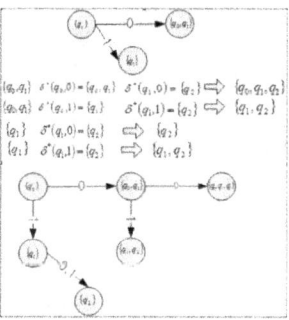

NFA → DFA

- NFA → DFA 3

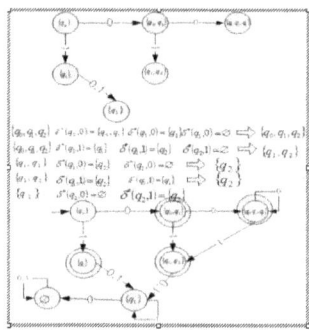

NFA → DFA

- Reduction of #States
  - If #States in NFA = Q
  - #States of DFA = $2^{|Q|}$
  - #Edges of DFA = $2^{|Q|}|\Sigma|$
  - Very Complicated Graph of DFA

Summary and Exercises

- Summary
  - State Transition Graphs as Graphical Representation of Finite Automata
  - Mathematical Definition and Characterization of DFA
  - Mathematical Definition and Characterization of NFA
  - NFA → DFA based on their Equivalence

Summary and Exercises

- Transition Graph <--> DFA

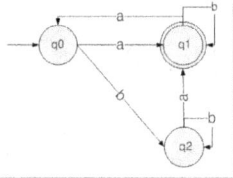
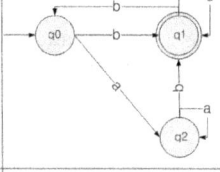
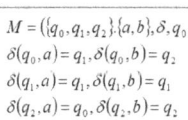

$M = (\{q_0,q_1,q_2\},\{a,b\},\delta,q_0,\{q_2\})$	$M = (\{q_0,q_1,q_2\},\{a,b\},\delta,q_0,\{q_0\})$
$\delta(q_0,a) = q_1, \delta(q_0,b) = q_2$	$\delta(q_0,a) = q_2, \delta(q_0,b) = q_1$
$\delta(q_1,a) = q_1, \delta(q_1,b) = q_1$	$\delta(q_1,a) = q_0, \delta(q_1,b) = q_2$
$\delta(q_2,a) = q_0, \delta(q_2,b) = q_2$	$\delta(q_2,a) = q_1, \delta(q_2,b) = q_2$

Summary and Exercises

- Language ---> DFA Alphabet={a,b}
  - String with the Prefix "ab"
  - String with the Substring "ab"
  - String with the Postfix "ab"
  - String not including "ab"

Summary and Exercises

- Transition Graph <---> NFA

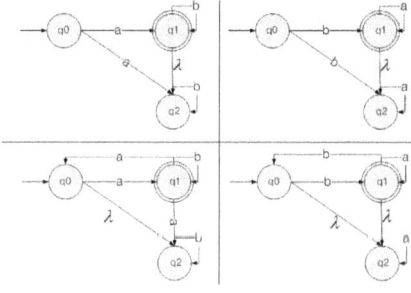

Summary and Exercises

- NFA ---> DFA

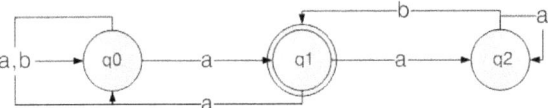

Regular Expression
Lecture 03

Outline

- Introduction
- Regular Expression
- Regular Grammar
- Example
- Summary and Exercises

Introduction

- Representation of Regular Language

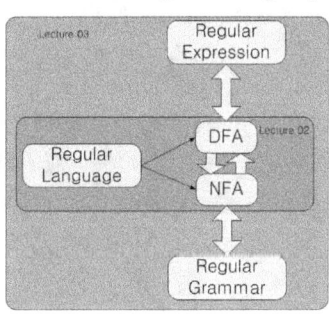

Introduction
- Regular Language ---> FA

String with Prefix "aab"

⬇

```
   ┌a→(q0)─a→(q1)─a→(q2)─b→((q3))↰a,b
              ╲    ╲   ╱
               b   b  a
                ╲  ↓ ╱
                 (q1)
                  ↺ a,b
```

Introduction

- FA ←→ Regular Language & Grammar

Regular Expression   Regular Grammar

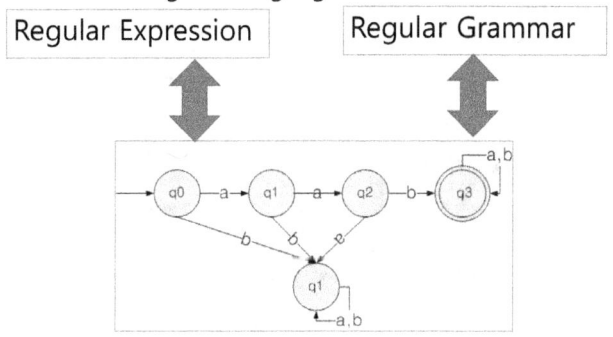

Introduction

- Regular Grammar vs Context Free Grammar

$G_2 = (\{S, S_1, S_2\}, \{a, b\}, S, P_2)$ $G = (\{S\}, \{a, b\}, S, P)$
$S \to S_1 ab, S_1 \to S_1 ab \mid S_2, S_2 \to a$ $S \to aSb, S \to \lambda$

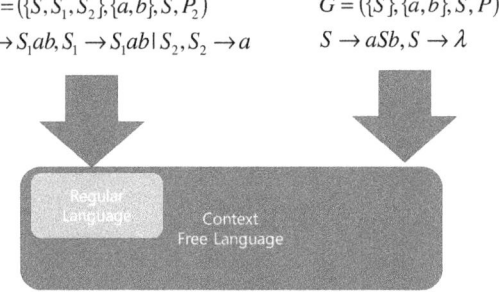

Introduction

- Goal of this Lecture
    - Regular Expression → Finite Accepter
    - Finite Accepter → Regular Expression
    - Regular Grammar → Finite Accepter
    - Finite Accepter → Regular Grammar

Regular Expression

- Definition of Regular Expression
    - Primitive Regular Expression: $\emptyset, \lambda, a \in \Sigma$
    - Regular Expressions r_1, r_2
        - $r_1 + r_2$ Regular Expression
        - $r_1 \cdot r_2$ Regular Expression
        - r_1^* Regular Expression
        - r_1 Regular Expression
- String ← Primitive Regular Expression by Rule 2
- Example:

$$a^* \cdot (a+b)$$

Regular Expression

- Regular Expression → Finite Accepter

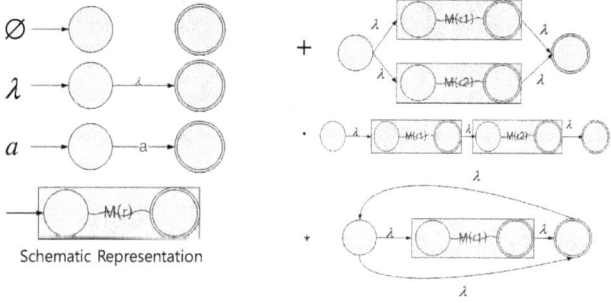

Schematic Representation

Regular Expression

- Finite Accepter →Regular Expression

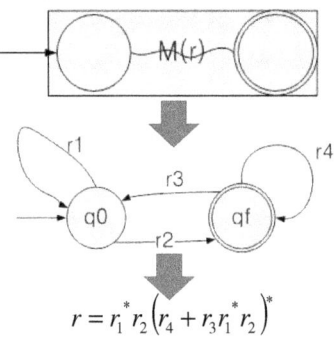

$$r = r_1^* r_2 (r_4 + r_3 r_1^* r_2)^*$$

Regular Expression

- Example: ab+a*

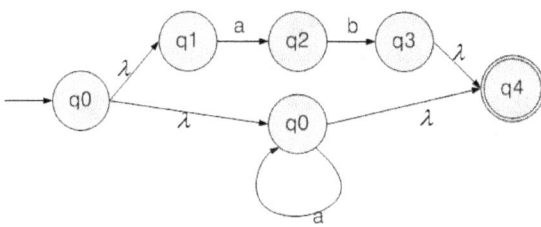

Regular Expression

- Comments on Regular Expression
  - Association of Regular Expression with Regular Language
    - Empty Set $\emptyset$
    - Empty String $\lambda \to \{\lambda\}$
    - Single Alphabet $a \to \{a\}$
    - Or $L(r_1 + r_2) = L(r_1) \cup L(r_2)$
    - Concatenation $L(r_1 \cdot r_2) = L(r_1)L(r_2)$
    - Repetition $L(r_1^*) = (L(r_1))^*$
    - Parenthesis $L((r_1)) = L(r_1)$
  - Precedence of Operators $\quad (\,) > * > \cdot > +$
  - Example $\quad L(a^* \cdot (a+b)) = L(a^*)L(a+b)$
    $= (L(a))^*(L(a) \cup L(b))$
    $= \{\lambda, a, aa, aaa, \ldots\}\{a, b\}$
    $= \{a, aa, aaa, \ldots, b, ab, aab, \ldots\}$
  - Regular Language → Regular Expression
    - 1. $L(r) = \{a^{2n}b^{3m+1} : n \geq 0, m \geq 0\} \quad r = (aa)^*(bb)^*b$
    - 2. $L(r) = \{w \in \Sigma^* : w \text{ has at least one pair of consecutive a's}\} \quad r = (a+b)^*aa(a+b)^*$

Regular Grammar

- Definition of Regular Grammar
    - Production Rule
        - A→xB: Right Linear Grammar
        - A→Bx: Left Linear Grammar
    - Single Variable in right side of each Production Rule in left most or right most

$$G_1 = (\{S\}, \{a,b\}, S, P_1) S \to abS \mid a$$
$$G_2 = (\{S, S_1, S_2\}, \{a,b\}, S, P_2)$$
$$S \to S_1 ab, S_1 \to S_1 ab \mid S_2, S_2 \to a$$

Regular Grammar

- Linear Right → Finite Accepter

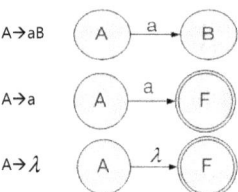

A→aB

A→a

A→λ

$$V_i \to a_1 a_2, ..., a_n V_j \quad \Longrightarrow \quad \delta^*(V_i, a_1 a_2, ..., a_n) = V_j$$
$$V_i \to a_1 a_2, ..., a_n \quad \Longrightarrow \quad \delta^*(V_i, a_1 a_2, ..., a_n) = V_f$$

Regular Grammar
- Finite Accepter → Linear Right
  - States → Variables
  - Initial State → Start Variable
  - Alphabet → Terminals:
  - Edge:
  - Final States:

$V = \{q_0, q_1, ..., q_n\}$

$\Sigma = T$

$\delta(q_i, a_j) = q_k \implies q_i \to a_j q_k$

$q_k \in F \implies q_k \to \lambda$

Regular Grammar

- Example

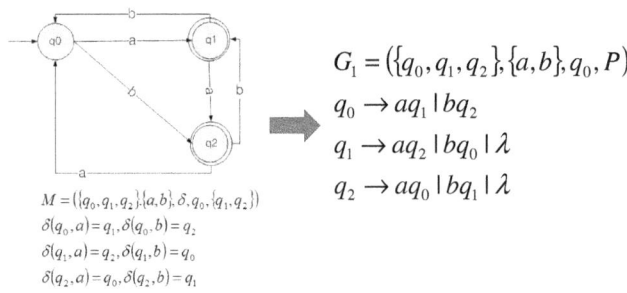

$M = (\{q_0, q_1, q_2\}, \{a, b\}, \delta, q_0, \{q_1, q_2\})$
$\delta(q_0, a) = q_1, \delta(q_0, b) = q_2$
$\delta(q_1, a) = q_2, \delta(q_1, b) = q_0$
$\delta(q_2, a) = q_0, \delta(q_2, b) = q_1$

$G_1 = (\{q_0, q_1, q_2\}, \{a, b\}, q_0, P)$
$q_0 \to aq_1 \mid bq_2$
$q_1 \to aq_2 \mid bq_0 \mid \lambda$
$q_2 \to aq_0 \mid bq_1 \mid \lambda$

Regular Grammar

- Comments on Regular Grammar
$$G = (\{S, A, B\}, \{a, b\}, S, P)$$
$$S \to A, A \to aB \mid \lambda, B \to Ab$$
  - Linear Grammar with Left and Right Linear
  - Never Regular Grammar
    - All Regular Languages → Linear Grammar
    - Not All Linear Grammar → Regular Languages

Example

- Examples: String consisting of 'a' and 'b'
  - String with Prefix "ab" → ab(a+b)*
  - String with Substring "ab" → (a+b)*ab(a+b)*
  - String with Postfix "ab" → (a+b)*ab
  - String not including "ab" → b*a*

Example

- Any String of Prefix "ab"

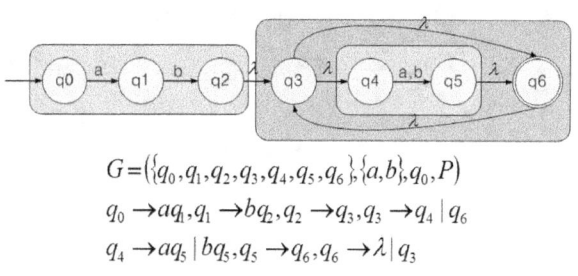

$G = (\{q_0, q_1, q_2, q_3, q_4, q_5, q_6\}, \{a, b\}, q_0, P)$
$q_0 \to aq_1, q_1 \to bq_2, q_2 \to q_3, q_3 \to q_4 \mid q_6$
$q_4 \to aq_5 \mid bq_5, q_5 \to q_6, q_6 \to \lambda \mid q_3$

Example

- Any String of Substring "ab"

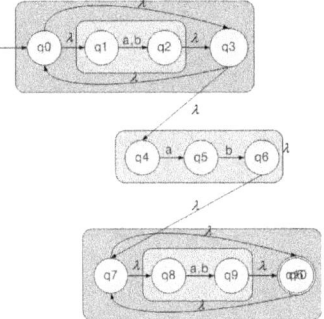

Example

- Any String of Postfix "ab"

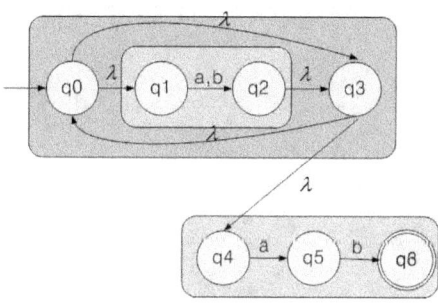

Example

- Any String not including "ab"

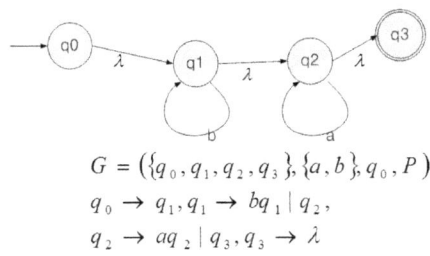

$G = (\{q_0, q_1, q_2, q_3\}, \{a, b\}, q_0, P)$
$q_0 \to q_1, q_1 \to bq_1 \mid q_2,$
$q_2 \to aq_2 \mid q_3, q_3 \to \lambda$

Summary and Exercises

- Summary
    - Representations of Regular Language: FA, RE, and RG
    - Regular Expression
        - Primitive Regular Expression: Empty Set, Empty String, and Single Alphabet
        - Operations: Or, Concatenation, Union, and Repetition
        - Regular Expression ←→ Finite Accepter
    - Regular Grammar ←→ Finite Accepter
    - Example: Four Types of Regular Languages
        - Regular Expression ←→ Finite Accepter
        - Regular Grammar ←→ Finite Accepter

Summary and Exercises

- Regular Expression → Finite Accepter
    - a + b
    - ab
    - a*b*
    - (ab)*

Summary and Exercises

- Finite Accepter → Regular Expression

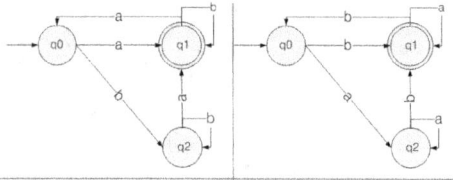

$M = (\{q_0, q_1, q_2\}, \{a, b\}, \delta, q_0, \{q_2\})$	$M = (\{q_0, q_1, q_2\}, \{a, b\}, \delta, q_0, \{q_0\})$
$\delta(q_0, a) = q_1, \delta(q_0, b) = q_2$	$\delta(q_0, a) = q_2, \delta(q_0, b) = q_1$
$\delta(q_1, a) = q_1, \delta(q_1, b) = q_1$	$\delta(q_1, a) = q_0, \delta(q_1, b) = q_2$
$\delta(q_2, a) = q_0, \delta(q_2, b) = q_2$	$\delta(q_2, a) = q_1, \delta(q_2, b) = q_2$

Summary and Exercises

- Linear Right → Finite Accepter

$$P: S \to A, A \to aB \mid \lambda, B \to b$$
$$P: S \to A, A \to abA \mid \lambda$$
$$P: S \to A, A \to bB, B \to bA \mid \lambda$$
$$P: S \to A, A \to aB, B \to bA \mid \lambda$$

Summary and Exercises

- Finite Accepter → Linear Right

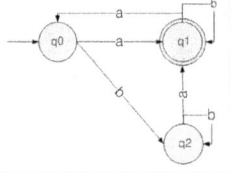 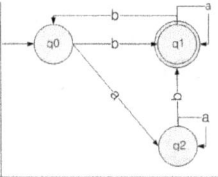

$M = (\{q_0,q_1,q_2\},\{a,b\},\delta,q_0,\{q_2\})$	$M = (\{q_0,q_1,q_2\},\{a,b\},\delta,q_0,\{q_0\})$
$\delta(q_0,a) = q_1, \delta(q_0,b) = q_2$	$\delta(q_0,a) = q_2, \delta(q_0,b) = q_1$
$\delta(q_1,a) = q_1, \delta(q_1,b) = q_1$	$\delta(q_1,a) = q_0, \delta(q_1,b) = q_2$
$\delta(q_2,a) = q_0, \delta(q_2,b) = q_2$	$\delta(q_2,a) = q_1, \delta(q_2,b) = q_2$

Regular Languages Properties
Lecture 04

Outline

- Questions about Regular Language
- Closure under Set Operations
- Closure under String Operations
- Identification of Nonregular Language
- Summary and Exercises

Questions about Regular Language

- Questions about Regular Languages
    - Scope and Characterization of Regular Languages
    - Language → Regular Language?
    - If so, is it empty, finite, or infinite?
    - Regular language 1 = Regular Language 2 ?

Questions about Regular Language

- Regular Language or Non-regular?
  - Alphabet and String $\quad w = \Sigma^*$
  - Using DFA
  - If reach a goal state, it is regular language
  - Otherwise, it is not

Questions about Regular Language

- Empty, Finite, or Infinite?
    - Regular Language → Transition Graph
    - If no path from the initial to a final state, it is empty string
    - If cycle in the path, it is infinite string
    - Otherwise, it is finite string

Questions about Regular Language

- Equality of Two Regular Languages
  - Two Regular Languages: and L_1 L_2
  - Equality? $L_1 = L_2$
  - If $L_3 = (L_1 \cap \overline{L_2}) \cup (\overline{L_1} \cap L_2)$ then $L_3 = \emptyset$ $L_1 = L_2$

Questions about Regular Language

- Goal of this Lecture
    - Ability to prove the Closure of Regular Language under Set Operations
    - Ability to prove the Closure of Regular Language under String Operations
    - Ability to identify Non-regular Language by using the Pigeonhole principle
    - Ability to identify Non-regular Language by using the Pumping Lemma

Closure under Set Operations

- Set Operations on Regular Languages
    - Regular Language → A Set
    - Apply Set Operations on Regular Languages
    - Apply String Operations on Regular Languages
    - Results from applying the Operations → Regular Language

Closure under Set Operations

- Closure under Four Operations

$$L(r_1 + r_2) = L(r_1) \cup L(r_2)$$
$$L(r_1 \cdot r_2) = L(r_1)L(r_2)$$
$$L(r_1^*) = (L(r_1))^*$$

$M = (Q, \Sigma, \delta, q_0, F)$ accepts L_1

⬇

$M = (Q, \Sigma, \delta, q_0, Q - F)$ accepts $\overline{L_1}$

Closure under Set Operations

- Closure under Intersection

$M = (Q, \Sigma, \delta_1, q_0, F_1)$ accepts L_1

$M = (P, \Sigma, \delta_2, p_0, F_2)$ accepts L_2

$\delta(q_i, a) = q_k$ and $\delta(p_j, a) = p_l$ $\implies$ $\hat{\delta}((q_i, p_j), a) = (q_k, p_l)$

$\hat{M} = (\hat{Q}, \Sigma, \hat{\delta}, (q_0, p_0), \hat{F})$

$p_i \in F_1$ and $p_i \in F_2$ $\implies$ $(p_i, q_j) \in \hat{F}$

Closure under Set Operations

- Closure under Difference

$$L_1 - L_2 = L_1 \cap \overline{L_2}$$

L_1 ⟹ Regular Language

$\overline{L_2}$ ⟹ Regular Language
   By closure under Complement

$L_1 \cap \overline{L_2}$ ⟹ Regular Language
   By closure under Intersection

Closure under Set Operations

- Closure under XOR

$$L_1 \oplus L_2 = (L_1 - L_2) \cup (L_2 - L_1)$$
$$L_1 \cap \overline{L_2} \implies \text{Regular Language}$$
$$L_2 \cap \overline{L_1} \implies \text{Regular Language}$$
$$(L_1 - L_2) \cup (L_2 - L_1) \implies \text{Regular Language}$$

Closure under String Operations

- Closure under Trivial String Operations
    - Closure under Concatenation $\quad L(r_1 \cdot r_2) = L(r_1)L(r_2)$
    - Closure under Repetition $\quad L(r_1^*) = (L(r_1))^*$
    - Closure under Repetition including Empty

- Closure under Reversal $\quad L(r_1^+) = (L(r_1))^*$
    - Multiple Final States → Single Final State
    - Single Final State → Initial State
    - Initial State → Final State

Closure under String Operations

- Definition of Homomorphism
  - Replacement of each Letter by a String in another Alphabet
  - $h: \Sigma \rightarrow \Gamma^*$ where Σ and Γ are alphabets
  - If $w = a_1 a_2 ... a_n$, $h(w) = h(a_1)h(a_2)...h(a_n)$
  - If L is a language, $h(L) = \{h(w): w \in L\}$

Closure under String Operations

- Example of Homomorphism

$$\Sigma = \{a,b\} \quad \Gamma = \{b,c,d\}$$
$$h(a) = dbcc, h(b) = bdc$$
$$r = (a+b)^*(aa)^*$$
$$r_1 = (dbcc+bdc)^*(dbccdbcc)^*$$

Closure under String Operations

- Closure under Homomorphism
  - If L is a regular language, $h(L)$ is also a regular language
  - $a \in \Sigma, h(a) = b_1, \ldots, b_n, b_i \in \Gamma$
  - $h(a)$, and b_i is regular
  - $h(r_1) + h(r_2) \quad h(r_1) \cdot h(r_2) \quad h(r_1^*) = (h(r_1))^*$

Closure under String Operations

- Closure under Other Operations
    - Closure under Prefix
    - Closure under Postfix
    - Closure under Suffix
    - Closure under removal of Substring

Identification of Non-regular Language

- Pigeonhole Principle

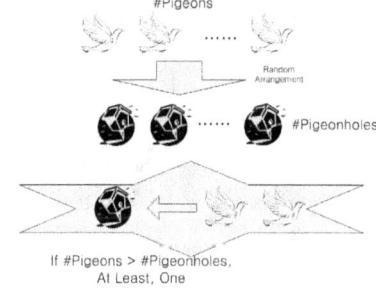

Identification of Non-regular Language

- Non-regular Language: $L = \{a^n b^n : n \geq 0\}$

$\delta^*(q_0, a^n b^n) = \delta^*(\delta^*(q_0, a^n), b^n) = \delta^*(q, b^n) = q_f \in F$

$\delta^*(q_0, a^i), i = 1, 2, \ldots\ |i| = \infty \rightarrow |i| > |Q|$

$\delta^*(q_0, a^m) = q, \delta^*(q_0, a^n) = q$, with $m \neq n$
By the Pigeonhole Principle

$\delta^*(q_0, a^m b^n) = \delta^*(\delta^*(q_0, a^m), b^n) = \delta^*(q, b^n) = q_f \in F$
➡ Contradiction!

Identification of Non-regular Language

- Pumping Lemma
  - Path Length > #States
  - Acceptance of Infinite Regular Language by a Cycle of Path
  - Decomposition of each String into the Three Parts
  - Another Strings by Repeating the Middle Parts in given Language

Identification of Non-regular Language

- Formal Definition of Pumping Lemma

$$\delta^*(q_0, w) = q_f \in F \quad |w| \geq path\_length$$

$$w = xyz, |y| = k \geq 1$$

$$\delta(q_0, x) = q_r \quad \delta(q_r, y) = q_r \quad \delta(q_0, xy^3z) = q_f$$

$$\delta(q_0, xz) = q_f \quad \delta(q_0, xy^2z) = q_f \quad \delta(q_r, z) = q_f$$

Identification of Non-regular Language

- $L = \{a^n b^n : n \geq 0\}$ By Pumping Lemma

$$a^n b^n = xyz$$
$$|y| = k \geq 1$$
$$w_0 = xz = a^{m-k} b^m \implies \text{Contradiction!}$$
$$w_0 = xz = a^m b^{m-k} \implies \text{Contradiction!}$$

Summary and Exercises

- Summary
  - Characterization of Regular Languages
  - Closure of Regular Languages under Set Operations
  - Closure of Regular Languages under String Operations
  - Identification of Non-regular Languages by Pigeonhole Principle and Pumping Lemma

Summary and Exercises

- Closure under Set Operations
  - Prove that $L_1 \cup L_2 \cup L_3$ is regular if L_1, L_2, L_3 are regular
  - Prove that $L_1 \cap L_2 \cap L_3$ is regular if L_1, L_2, L_3 are regular
  - Prove by Induction that $\bigcup_{i=1}^{n} L_i$ is regular if $L_1, ..., L_n$ are regular
  - Prove by Induction that $\bigcap_{i=1}^{n} L_i$ is regular if $L_1, ..., L_n$ are regular

Summary and Exercises

- Map the DFA into one applied by Homomorphism

$\Sigma = \{a, b\}$
$\Gamma = \{b, c, d\}$

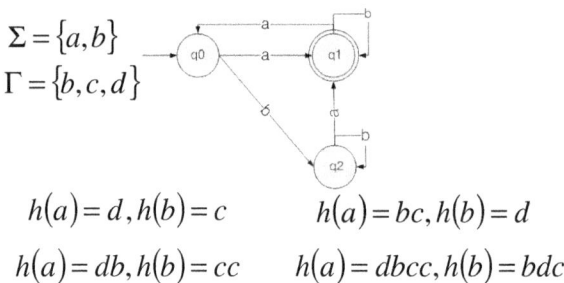

$h(a) = d, h(b) = c$ $h(a) = bc, h(b) = d$

$h(a) = db, h(b) = cc$ $h(a) = dbcc, h(b) = bdc$

Summary and Exercises

- $L = \{a^{2n}b^{2n} : n \geq 1\}$ → Non Regular Language by the Pigeonhole Principle

Summary and Exercises

- $L = \{a^{2n}b^{2n} : n \geq 1\}$ → Non Regular Language by the Pumping Lemma

Context Free Languages
Lecture 05

Outline

- Introduction
- Derivations
- Exhaustive Search Parsing
- Ambiguity
- Summary and Exercises

Introduction

- Definition of Context Free Language
  - $G = (V, T, S, P)$ as Context Free Grammar
  - $A \xrightarrow{\text{where}} x$ and $A \in V$, $x \in (V \cup T)^*$
- L: Contest Free Language
  - L = L(G)
  - G: Context Free Grammar
- Regular Grammar as Subset of Context Free Grammar

Introduction

- Example 1 of Context Free Language
  - Language $L(G) = \{ww^R : w \in \{a,b\}^*\}$
  - aabbaa, aaaaa, bbaaaabb, ….
  - Grammar
  - Production $G = (\{S\}, \{a,b\}, S, P)$

  $S \to aSa, S \to bSb, S \to \lambda$

Introduction

- Example 2 of Context Free Language
  - Language $\quad L(G) = \{ab(bbaa)^n bba(ba)^n : n \geq 0\}$
  - abbba, abbbaabba, abbbaba, ...
  - Grammar
  - Production $\quad G = (\{S, A, B\}, \{a, b\}, S, P)$
    $S \rightarrow abB, A \rightarrow aaBb, B \rightarrow bbAa, A \rightarrow \lambda$

Introduction

- Example 3 of Context Free Language
  - Language $\quad L(G) = \{a^n b^m : m \neq n\}$
  - abb, aab, aaaabbb,...
  - Grammar:
  - Production $\quad G = (\{S, S_1, A, B\}, \{a, b\}, S, P)$

$$S \to AS_1 \mid S_1 B, S_1 \to aS_1 b \mid \lambda, A \to aA \mid a, B \to bB \mid b$$

Introduction

- Goal of this Lecture
  - Survey Examples of Context Free Language
  - Obtain Schemes of Deriving Sentences by Grammar
  - Obtain how to parse Sentences for deciding their Memberships
  - Observe Ambiguity of Context Free Language

Derivations

- Definition of Derivation

$$G = (V, T, S, P)$$

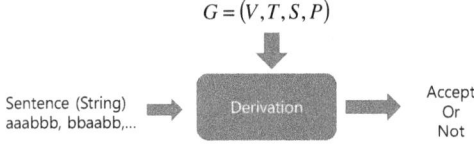

Sentence (String) aaabbb, bbaabb,... → Derivation → Accept Or Not

Derivations

- Example 01

$$G = (\{A,B,S\},\{a,b\},S,P)$$

$$S \to AB, A \to aaA, A \to \lambda, B \to Bb, B \to \lambda$$

$$S \Rightarrow AB \Rightarrow aaAB \Rightarrow aaB \Rightarrow aaBb \Rightarrow aab$$

$$S \Rightarrow AB \Rightarrow ABb \Rightarrow ABBb \Rightarrow aaAb \Rightarrow aab$$

Derivations

- Example 02

$$G = (\{A, B, S\}, \{a, b\}, S, P)$$

$$S \rightarrow aAB, A \rightarrow bBb, B \rightarrow A \mid \lambda$$

$S \Rightarrow aAB \Rightarrow abBbB \Rightarrow abAbB \Rightarrow abbBbbB \Rightarrow abbbbB \Rightarrow abbbb$

$S \Rightarrow aAB \Rightarrow aA \Rightarrow abAb \Rightarrow abbBbb \Rightarrow abbbb$

Derivations

- Derivation Tree
  - Non-Leaf Nodes
    - Root Node ← S (Start Symbol)
    - Interior Nodes ← Variables
  - Leaf Nodes ← $T \cup \{\lambda\}$
  - Production:
    - Node ← $A \rightarrow a_1, a_2, ..., a_n$, $A \in V$
    - Child Nodes ← $a_1 a_2, ..., a_n$
  - Leaf Node ← λ : No Sibling

Derivations

- Sentential Form ←→ Derivation Tree
$G = (\{A, B, S\}, \{a, b\}, S, P)$

$S \rightarrow aAB, A \rightarrow bBb, B \rightarrow A \mid \lambda$

abbbb

Exhaustive Search Parsing

- Overview of Exhaustive Search Parsing
  - Membership Algorithm
    - Decision whether the sentence belongs to the language or not in Context Free Language
  - Parsing
    - Derive the Sentence by the Given Grammar
    - A Sequence of Production Rules as Output
  - Exhaustive Search Parsing in each Round
    - Generate all Possible Production Rules
    - Select Production Rules partially or entirely matching the Sentence
  - Need to Remove the Production Rules for Efficiency
    - Parse the A with two $found$ B

Exhaustive Search Parsing

- Example 1 of Exhaustive Search Parsing

$$S \rightarrow SS \mid aSb \mid bSa \mid \lambda, w = aabb$$

$$S \Rightarrow SS, S \Rightarrow aSb, S \Rightarrow bSa, S \Rightarrow \lambda$$

$S \Rightarrow SS \Rightarrow SSS$	$S \Rightarrow aSb \Rightarrow aSSb$
$S \Rightarrow SS \Rightarrow aSbS$	$S \Rightarrow aSb \Rightarrow aaSbb$
$S \Rightarrow SS \Rightarrow bSaS$	$S \Rightarrow aSb \Rightarrow abSab$
$S \Rightarrow SS \Rightarrow S$	$S \Rightarrow aSb \Rightarrow ab$

$$S \Rightarrow aSb \Rightarrow aaSbb \Rightarrow aabb$$

Exhaustive Search Parsing

- Example 2 of Exhaustive Search Parsing

$$S \to SS \mid aSb \mid bSa \mid ab \mid ba, w = aabb$$

$S \Rightarrow SS \Rightarrow SSS$ $\qquad S \Rightarrow aSb \Rightarrow aSSb$

$S \Rightarrow SS \Rightarrow aSbS$ $\qquad S \Rightarrow aSb \Rightarrow aaSbb$

$S \Rightarrow SS \Rightarrow bSaS$ $\qquad S \Rightarrow aSb \Rightarrow abSab$

$S \Rightarrow SS \Rightarrow abS$ $\qquad \boxed{S \Rightarrow aSb \Rightarrow aabb}$

$S \Rightarrow SS \Rightarrow baS$ $\qquad S \Rightarrow aSb \Rightarrow abab$

Exhaustive Search Parsing

- Example 3 of Exhaustive Search Parsing

$$G = (\{A, B, S\}, \{a, b\}, S, P)$$
$$S \rightarrow aAB, A \rightarrow bBb, B \rightarrow A \mid \lambda$$
$$S \rightarrow aAA, A \rightarrow bAb, A \rightarrow bb$$
$$S \Rightarrow aAA \Rightarrow abbA \Rightarrow abbbb$$

Exhaustive Search Parsing

- S-Grammar

$$G = (V, T, S, P) \quad A \to ax$$

$A \in V, a \in T, x \in V^*$ (A, a) Only One Time in Production Rules

$S \to aAA, A \to bAb, A \to bb$ Non S Grammar

$S \to aAA, A \to Abb, A \to bb$ S Grammar

Ambiguity

- Overview of Ambiguity
  - Interpretation of a Sentence into two or more Meanings
  - 2 + 3 * 5, if put no precedence over operations
    - (2 + 3) * 5 = 25
    - 2 + (3 * 5) = 30
  - Two ore More Derivation Trees to a Sentence
  - Need Disambiguation

Ambiguity

- Example 1 of Ambiguity

    $S \rightarrow aSb \mid SS \mid \lambda$ aabb

Ambiguity

- Example 2 of Ambiguity

$G = (V,T,E,P)$ $V = \{E, I\}$ $T = \{a,b,c,+,*,(,)\}$

$E \to I, E \to E+E, E \to E*E, E \to (E), I \to a \mid b \mid c$

a + b * c

Ambiguity

- Disambiguation of Example 2

$G = (V, T, E, P)$ $V = \{E, T, F, I\}$ $T = \{a, b, c, +, *, (,)\}$

$E \rightarrow T$
$T \rightarrow F$
$F \rightarrow I$
$E \rightarrow E + T$
$T \rightarrow T * F$
$F \rightarrow (E)$
$I \rightarrow a \mid b \mid c$

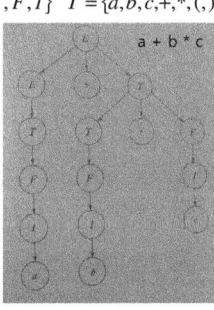

a + b * c

Ambiguity

- Inherently Ambiguous Context Free Language

$$L = \{a^n b^n c^m\} \cup \{a^n b^m c^m\}$$
$$L = L_1 \cup L_2$$
$L_1 \quad S_1 \rightarrow S_1 c \mid A, A \rightarrow aAb \mid \lambda$
$L_2 \quad S_2 \rightarrow aS_2 \mid B, B \rightarrow bBc \mid \lambda$

$a^n b^n c^n$ Derived from either of both Grammars

Summary and Exercises

- Summary
  - Survey of Some Examples of Context Free Languages
  - Derivation Schemes
    - Leftmost Derivation
    - Rightmost Derivation
    - Derivation Tree
  - Exhaustive Search Parsing as Membership Algorithm
  - Ambiguity in Grammar or Language

Summary and Exercises

- Leftmost & Rightmost Derivation
  $G = (\{S\}, \{a,b\}, S, P)$
  $$S \to aSa, S \to bSb, S \to \lambda$$
  leftmost derivation
      abba, abbaabba, babbbbab, and aaaabbaaaa

  rightmost derivation
      abba, abbaabba, babbbbab, and aaaabbaaaa

Summary and Exercises

- Derivation Tree

$$G = (\{S, S_1, A, B\}, \{a,b\}, S, P)$$
$S \to AS_1 \mid S_1B, S_1 \to aS_1b \mid \lambda, A \to aA \mid a, B \to bB \mid b$

Draw Derivation Tree to aaaabbb
Draw Derivation Tree to aaabbbb

Summary and Exercises

- Exhaustive Search Parsing

   $S \to abB, A \to aaBb, B \to bbAa, A \to \lambda$

   Exhaustive Search Parsing to abbba and abbbaabba

   Conversion of above into s-Grammar

   Exhaustive Search Parsing to abbba and abbbaabba By S-Grammar

Summary and Exercises

- Ambiguity or Not?

    $S \to aSb \mid SS \mid \lambda$ aaabbb

Context Free Grammar Simplification
Lecture 06

Outline

- Introduction
- Removal of λ-Production
- Removal of Useless Production
- Chomsky Normal Form
- Summary and Exercises

Introduction

- Transformation of Context Free Grammar

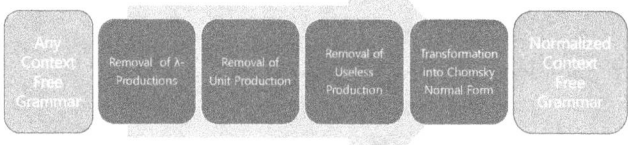

Introduction

- Assumption of No Empty String

  $G = (V, T, S, P)$ Context Free Grammar of L

  $\hat{G} = (\hat{V}, \hat{T}, \hat{S}, \hat{P})$ Context Free Grammar of $L - \{\lambda\}$

  $L(\hat{G}) = L(G) - \{\lambda\}$

  $\hat{P} + (S_0 \to S \mid \lambda) \to P$

Introduction

- Substitution Rule

    Simplification of Grammar by the Substitution Rule

    $A \to x_1 B x_2 \quad B \to y_1 \mid y_2 \mid ... \mid y_n$

    $S \stackrel{*}{\Rightarrow}_G u_1 A u_2 \Rightarrow_G u_1 x_1 B x_2 u_2 \Rightarrow_G u_1 x_1 y_i x_2 u_2$

    $A \to x_1 y_1 x_2 \mid x_1 y_2 x_2 \mid ... \mid x_1 y_n x_2$

    $S \stackrel{*}{\Rightarrow}_{\hat{G}} u_1 A u_2 \Rightarrow_{\hat{G}} u_1 x_1 y_i x_2 u_2$

Introduction

- Example of Substitution Rule

$$G = (\{A, B\}, \{a, b, c\}, A, P)$$
$$A \to a \mid aaA \mid abBc$$
$$B \to abbA \mid b$$

$$G = (\{A\}, \{a, b, c\}, A, P)$$
$$A \to a \mid aaA \mid ababbAc \mid abbc$$

Introduction

- Goal of this Lecture
  - Transform CFG into its more efficient Version
  - Transform CFG into the Version without λ-Production
  - Transform CFG into the Version without Unit Production and Useless Production
  - Transform CFG into Chomsky Normal Form

Removal of λ-Production

- λ-Production and Nullable Variables

  $A \to \lambda$ ⟹ λ-Production
  $A \to a \mid aaA \mid \lambda$

  $A \overset{*}{\Rightarrow} \lambda$ ⟹ Nullable Production
  $A \to A_1 A_2 ... A_n$
  $A_i \to \lambda$

Removal of λ-Production

- Select Nullable Variables

$V_N = \emptyset$ ⟹ Initialization of Set of Nullable Variables

$A \in V_N \quad A \to \lambda$ ⟹ Variables of λ-Production

$B \in V_N \quad B \to A_1 A_2, ..., A_n \in (V_N \cup T)$

No λ-Production ⟹ No Nullable Variable

Removal of λ-Production

- Combination and Deletion
    Deletion of all λ-Productions
    Generation of All Combinations of Nullable Variables
    $V_N = \{A, B, C\}$
    A, B, C, AB, AC, BC, and ABC

Removal of λ-Production

- Addition of More Production

$V_N = \{A, B, C\}$ $\qquad$ $S \rightarrow ABaC \mid BaC \mid AaC \mid ABa \mid$
$S \rightarrow ABaC$ $\qquad\qquad$ $aC \mid Ba \mid Aa \mid a$
$A \rightarrow BC$ $\qquad\qquad$ $A \rightarrow B \mid C \mid BC \mid \cancel{\lambda}$

Removal of λ-Production

- Example

$V_n = \{A, B, C\}$

$S \to ABaC$
$A \to BC$
$B \to b \mid \lambda$
$C \to D \mid \lambda$
$D \to d$

A, B, C, AB, AC, BC, and ABC

$S \to ABaC$
$A \to BC$
$B \to b$
$C \to D$
$D \to d$

$S \to ABaC \mid BaC \mid AaC \mid ABa \mid aC \mid Ba \mid Aa \mid a$
$A \to B \mid C \mid BC$
$B \to b$
$C \to D$
$D \to d$

Removal of Useless Production

- Undesirable Productions
    - λ-Productions
    - Unit Productions
    - Non Terminal Productions
    - Non Reachable Productions

Removal of Useless Production

- Removal of Unit Production

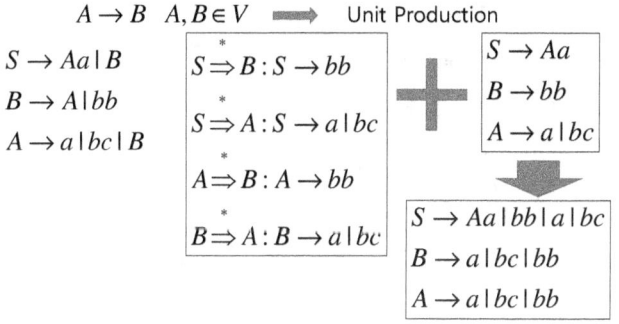

Removal of Useless Production

- Removal of Non Terminal Production

$V_1 = \emptyset$ Initialization of Set of Terminal Symbols

Repetition until no more Symbols

if $A \to x_1 x_2 ... x_n \in (V_1 \cup T)$

$V_1 \leftarrow V_1 \cup \{A\}$

$P_1 \leftarrow P_1 \cup \{A \to x_1 x_2 ... x_n\}$

$G = (\{S, A, B, C\}, \{a, b\}, S, P)$
$S \to aS \mid Ab \mid Cb$
$A \to a$
$B \to aa$
$C \to aCb$

$V_1 = \{S, A, B\}$
$G = (\{S, A, B\}, \{a\}, S, P)$
$S \to aS \mid A \mid$
$A \to a$
$B \to aa$

Removal of Useless Production

- Removal of Not Reachable Production

  Variable which we can not reach from the Start Symbol

  $G = (\{S, A, B\}, \{a\}, S, P)$
  $S \rightarrow aS \mid A \mid$
  $A \rightarrow a$
  $B \rightarrow aa$

  $\Longrightarrow$

  $G = (\{S, A, B\}, \{a\}, S, P)$
  $S \rightarrow aS \mid A \mid$
  $A \rightarrow a$

Removal of Useless Production

- Example

$S \to AB \mid Aa \mid Ba$
$A \to aa \mid B \mid \lambda$
$B \to bb \mid C \mid \lambda$
$C \to ccB \mid A$
$D \to cc$

$\Rightarrow$

$S \to AB \mid Aa \mid Ba \mid B \mid a \mid A$
$A \to aa \mid B$
$B \to bb \mid C$
$C \to ccB \mid A$
$D \to cc$

$\Downarrow$

$S \to AB \mid Aa \mid Ba \mid bb \mid a \mid aa \mid cc$
$A \to aa \mid bb \mid cc$
$B \to bb \mid aa \mid cc$
$C \to ccB \mid aa \mid bb$

$\Leftarrow$

$S \to AB \mid Aa \mid Ba \mid bb \mid a \mid aa \mid cc$
$A \to aa \mid bb \mid cc$
$B \to bb \mid aa \mid cc$
$C \to ccB \mid aa \mid bb$
$D \to cc$

Chomsky Normal Form

- Definition of Chomsky Normal Form

$A \to BC \in V$ and $A \to a \in T$ ➡ Chomsky Normal Form

$S \to AS \mid a$
$A \to SA \mid b$ ➡ Chomsky Normal Form

$S \to AS \mid AAS$
$A \to SA \mid aa$ ➡ Not Chomsky Normal Form

Chomsky Normal Form

- Preparation of Input Context Free Grammar

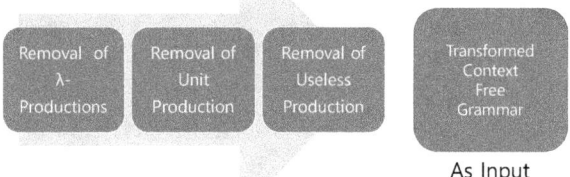

As Input

Chomsky Normal Form

- Intermediate Context Free Grammar

$$G = (V, T, S, P) \Longrightarrow G_1 = (V_1, T_1, S, P_1) \quad P_1 = \varnothing$$

$$P_1 \leftarrow P_1 \cup \{A \to a\}$$

$$\begin{matrix} A \to x_1 x_2 \ldots x_n \\ \forall x_i \in V \end{matrix} \Longrightarrow P_1 \leftarrow P_1 \cup \{A \to x_1 x_2 \ldots x_n\} n \geq 2$$

$$\begin{matrix} A \to x_1 x_2 \ldots x_n \\ \exists x_i \in T \end{matrix}$$

$$P_1 \leftarrow P_1 \cup \{A \to x_1 \ldots B_\alpha \ldots x_n, B_\alpha \leftarrow x_i\} n \geq 2$$

Chomsky Normal Form

- Chomsky Normal Form

$$G_1 = (V_1, T_1, S, P_1) \implies \hat{G} = (\hat{V}, \hat{T}, \hat{S}, \hat{P})$$

$$A \to x_1 x_2 \ldots x_n \in V$$
$$A \to x_1 D_1$$
$$D_1 \to x_2 D_2$$
$$\vdots$$
$$D_{n-2} \to x_{n-2} D_{n-2}$$

Chomsky Normal Form

- Example

$S \to ABa$
$A \to aab$
$B \to Ac$

$\Rightarrow$

$S \to ABB_a$
$A \to B_a B_a B_b$
$B \to AB_c$
$B_a \to a$
$B_b \to b$
$B_c \to c$

$\Rightarrow$

$S \to AD_1$
$D_1 \to BB_a$
$A \to B_a D_2$
$D_2 \to B_a B_b$
$B \to AB_c$
$B_a \to a$
$B_b \to b$
$B_c \to c$

Summary and Exercises

- Summary
  - Transformation by Substitution Rule as Basis
  - Transformation by Removing λ-Productions
  - Transformation by Removing Unit Productions and Useless Productions
  - Transformation into Chomsky Normal Form

Summary and Exercises
• Removal of λ-Productions

Ex01-01
$S \to Aa$
$A \to ab \mid \lambda$

Ex01-02
$S \to Aa$
$A \to ab \mid Bb$
$B \to bb \mid \lambda$

Ex01-03
$S \to Aa \mid AB$
$A \to ab \mid Bb \mid \lambda$
$B \to bb \mid \lambda$

Ex01-04
$S \to AB \mid Aa \mid Ba \mid A \mid B$
$A \to aa \mid B \mid C \mid \lambda$
$B \to bb \mid C \mid \lambda$
$C \to ccB \mid A$
$D \to cc$

Summary and Exercises

- Removal of Unit-Productions

Ex02-01
$S \to A$
$A \to aa$

Ex02-02
$S \to Aa \mid Bb$
$A \to B$
$B \to bb$

Ex02-03
$S \to Aa \mid Bb$
$A \to B$
$B \to bb \mid A$

Ex02-04
Remove Unit-Productions in the CFG
after removing λ-Productions in Exercise 01-04

Summary and Exercises

- Removal of Useless Productions

Ex03-01
$S \to Ab \mid aa$
$A \to aaS$

Ex03-02
$S \to Ab \mid aa$
$A \to aa \mid aaS$
$B \to bbA$

Ex03-03
$S \to Ab \mid aa$
$A \to aa \mid aaC$
$B \to bbA$
$C \to aaB$

Ex03-04
Remove Useless Productions in the CFG
after removing Unit Productions in Exercise 02-04

Summary and Exercises

- Chomsky Normal Form

    Ex04-01
    $S \to aba$

    Ex04-02
    $S \to abABa$
    $A \to bb$
    $B \to aa$

    Ex04-03
    $S \to abABa$
    $A \to bb$
    $B \to a$

    Ex04-04
    Transform the CFG into Chomsky Normal Form
    after removing Useless Productions in Exercise 03-04

Pushdown Automata

Lecture 07

Outline

- Introduction
- Acceptance of CFL
- CFG → Pushdown Automata
- Pushdown Automata → CFG
- Summary and Exercises

Introduction

- Overview of Pushdown Automata
  - The Class of Automata associated with Context Free Language
  - Addition of Stack to Finite State Automata
  - No Equivalence between Deterministic and Nondeterministic
  - Deterministic Context Free Language as a Proper Subset of Context Free Language

Introduction

- Schematic Representation

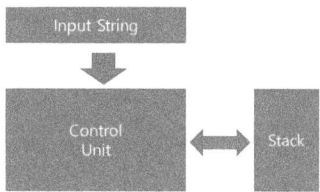

Introduction

- Formal Definition of Pushdown Automata

$$M = (Q, \Sigma, \Gamma, \delta, q_0, z, F)$$

Σ Input Alphabet Γ Stack Alphabet

δ Transition Function $Q \times (\Sigma \cup \{\lambda\}) \times \Gamma \to Q \times \Gamma^*$

z Stack Start Symbol

Introduction

- Example of Pushdown Automata

$$M = (Q, \Sigma, \Gamma, \delta, q_0, z, F)$$

$Q = \{q_0, q_1, q_2, q_3\}$ $\delta(q_0, a, 0) = \{(q_1, 10), (q_3, \lambda)\}$

$\Sigma = \{a, b\}$ $\delta(q_0, \lambda, 0) = \{(q_3, \lambda)\}$

$\Gamma = \{0, 1\}$ $\delta(q_1, a, 1) = \{(q_1, 11)\}$

$z = 0$ $\delta(q_1, b, 1) = \{(q_2, \lambda)\}$

$F = \{q_3\}$ $\delta(q_2, b, 1) = \{(q_2, \lambda)\}$

   $\delta(q_2, \lambda, 0) = \{(q_3, \lambda)\}$

$\delta(q_0, b, 0) = \varnothing$ Dead Configuration

Introduction

- Goal of this Lecture
  - Understand another type of Automata called Pushdown Automata accepting Context Free Language
  - Understand the Process of Converting Context Free Grammar into Pushdown Automata
  - Understand the Process of Converting Pushdown Automata into Context Free Grammar
  - Distinguish the Deterministic Pushdown Automata from Non-deterministic One

Acceptance of CFL

- Formal Definition of Acceptance

$$L(M) = \left\{ w \in \Sigma^* : (q_0, w, z) \vdash_M^* (q_f, \lambda, u), q_f \in F, u \in \Gamma^* \right\}$$

$$(q_2, y) \in \delta(q_1, a, b) \implies (q_1, aw, bx) \vdash (q_2, w, yx)$$

- $\vdash^*$ Arbitrary Number of Steps
- $\vdash_M$ Transfer by Automaton, M

Reach the Final State by reading w
Not Care whatever string is given in the stack

Acceptance of CFL

$$L = \{a^n b^n : n \geq 0\}$$

$$M = (\{q_0, q_1, q_2\}, \{a,b\}, \{0,1\}, \delta, q_0, 0, \{q_0\})$$

$$\delta(q_0, a, 0) = \{(q_1, 10)\}$$

$$\delta(q_1, a, 1) = \{(q_1, 11)\}$$

$$\delta(q_1, b, 1) = \{(q_2, \lambda)\}$$

$$\delta(q_2, b, 1) = \{(q_2, \lambda)\}$$

$$\delta(q_2, \lambda, 0) = \{(q_0, \lambda)\}$$

$(q_0, ab, 0) \vdash (q_1, b, 10) \vdash (q_2, \lambda, 0) \vdash (q_0, \lambda, \lambda)$

$(q_0, aabb, 0) \vdash (q_1, abb, 10) \vdash (q_1, bb, 110)$

$\vdash (q_2, b, 10) \vdash (q_2, \lambda, 0) \vdash (q_0, \lambda, \lambda)$

Acceptance of CFL

$$L = \{w \in \{a,b\}^* : n_a(w) = n_b(w)\}$$
$$M = (\{q_0, q_f\}, \{a,b\}, \{0,1,z\}, \delta, q_0, z, \{q_f\})$$

$\delta(q_0, \lambda, z) = \{(q_f, z)\}$ $\qquad (q_0, ab, z) \vdash (q_0, b, 0z) \vdash (q_0, \lambda, z)$
$\delta(q_0, a, z) = \{(q_0, 0z)\}$ $\qquad \vdash (q_f, \lambda, \lambda)$
$\delta(q_0, b, z) = \{(q_0, 1z)\}$
$\delta(q_0, a, 0) = \{(q_0, 00)\}$ $\qquad (q_0, baab, z) \vdash (q_0, aab, 1z) \vdash (q_0, ab, z)$
$\delta(q_0, b, 0) = \{(q_0, \lambda)\}$ $\qquad \vdash (q_0, b, 0z) \vdash (q_0, \lambda, z) \vdash (q_f, \lambda, z)$
$\delta(q_0, a, 1) = \{(q_0, \lambda)\}$
$\delta(q_0, b, 1) = \{(q_0, 11)\}$

Acceptance of CFL

$$L = \{ww^R : w \in \{a,b\}^+\}$$

$$M = (\{q_0, q_1, q_2\}, \{a,b\}, \{a,b,z\}, \delta, q_0, z, \{q_2\})$$

$\delta(q_0,a,a) = \{(q_0,aa)\}$ $\delta(q_0,\lambda,a) = \{(q_1,a)\}$ $\delta(q_1,a,a) = \{(q_1,\lambda)\}$ $\delta(q_1,\lambda,z) = \{(q_2,z)\}$
$\delta(q_0,a,b) = \{(q_0,ab)\}$ $\delta(q_0,\lambda,b) = \{(q_1,b)\}$ $\delta(q_1,b,b) = \{(q_1,\lambda)\}$
$\delta(q_0,b,a) = \{(q_0,ba)\}$
$\delta(q_0,b,b) = \{(q_0,bb)\}$
$\delta(q_0,a,z) = \{(q_0,az)\}$
$\delta(q_0,b,z) = \{(q_0,bz)\}$ (q_0,aa,z) (q_0,a,az) (q_1,a,az) (q_1,λ,z) (q_2,λ,z)

$(q_0,abba,z)$ (q_0,bba,az) (q_0,ba,baz) (q_1,ba,baz) (q_1,a,az) (q_1,λ,z) (q_2,λ,z)

Acceptance of CFL

- Deterministic PDA

<small>Only Single Element to each Transition Function</small> $\delta(q,a,b)$

$\delta(q_0,a,0) = \{(q_1,10),(q_3,\lambda)\}$ (**X**)

$\delta(q,\lambda,b) \neq \varnothing \implies \delta(q,c,b) = \varnothing \quad \forall c \in \Sigma$

$\delta(q_0,a,a) = \{(q_0,aa)\} \, \delta(q_0,\lambda,a) = \{(q_1,a)\}$ (**X**)

CFG → Pushdown Automata

- Definition of CFG → PDA

$$G = (V, T, S, P)$$
$$M = (\{q_0, q_1, q_f\}, T, V \cup \{z\}, \delta, q_0, z, \{q_f\})$$
$$S \implies \delta(q_0, \lambda, z) = \{(q_1, Sz)\}$$
$$\delta(q_1, \lambda, z) = \{(q_f, z)\} \quad \text{For Final State}$$
$$(q_1, u) \in \delta(q_1, a, A) \quad \text{For Productions}$$

CFG → Pushdown Automata

- Greibach Normal Form

  Context Free Grammar with all Productions with the following Form

  $A \to ax$ where $a \in T$ and $x \in V^*$

  $S \to aAB, A \to aB, B \to b$ Greichbach Normal Form

  $S \to AB, A \to abB, B \to bc$ Non Greichbach Normal Form

CFG → Pushdown Automata
- Conversion into Greibach Normal Form

$S \to AB$ $S \to aB$ $S \to aAbB$ $S \to aS_1S_2$
$A \to a$ ⟹ $B \to b$ $A \to a$ ⟹ $S_1 \to a$
$B \to b$ $B \to b$ $S_2 \to bB$
                                                $B \to b$

$S \to aaAB$ $S \to aS_1$ $S \to ABba$ $S \to aBS_1S_2$
$A \to a$ ⟹ $S_1 \to aAB$ $A \to a$ ⟹ $B \to b$
$B \to b$ $A \to a$ $B \to b$ $S_1 \to b$
                $B \to b$ $S_2 \to a$

CFG → Pushdown Automata

- Example in Greibach Normal Form

$S \to aAB, A \to aB, B \to b$

$M = (\{q_0, q_1, q_f\}, \{a, b\}, \{S, A, B, z\}, \delta, q_0, z, \{q_f\})$

$\delta(q_0, \lambda, z) = \{(q_1, Sz)\} \quad \delta(q_1, \lambda, z) = \{(q_f, z)\}$

$\delta(q_1, a, S) = \{(q_1, AB)\}$

$\delta(q_1, a, A) = \{(q_1, B)\}$

$\delta(q_1, b, B) = \{(q_1, \lambda)\}$

CFG → Pushdown Automata

- Example in non Greibach Normal Form

$S \to aSbb \mid a$ ⟹ $S \to aSA \mid a$
$A \to bB$
$B \to b$

$M = (\{q_0, q_1, q_f\}, \{a, b\}, \{S, A, B, z\}, \delta, q_0, z, \{q_f\})$

$\delta(q_0, \lambda, z) = \{(q_1, Sz)\} \quad \delta(q_1, \lambda, z) = \{(q_2, \lambda)\}$
$\delta(q_1, a, S) - \{(q_1, SA), (q_1, \lambda)\}$
$\delta(q_1, b, A) = \{(q_1, B)\} \quad \delta(q_1, b, B) = \{(q_1, \lambda)\}$

Pushdown Automata → CFG

- Requirements of PDA

    Req 1 Only Single Final State in Empty Stack

    $$(q_f, \lambda) \in \delta(q_i, \lambda, z)$$

    Req 2 Increment or Decrement in Stack

    $$\delta(q_j, a, A) = \{c_1, c_2, ..., c_n\}$$

    $$c_i = (q_j, \lambda)$$
    Or
    $$c_i = (q_j, BC)$$

    $(q_j, A) \in \delta(q_i, a, A)$ (**X**)

Pushdown Automata → CFG

- Variables and Productions

$(q_0 z q_f)$ Start Symbol
Remove z from the Stack in reading w $q_0 \to q_f$

$(q_i A q_j)$ Other symbols
Remove A from the Stack in reading w $q_i \to q_j$

$(q_j, \lambda) \in \delta(q_i, a, A) \implies (q_i A q_j) \to a$

$(q_k, BC) \in \delta(q_i, a, A) \implies (q_i A q_k) \to a(q_j B q_l)(q_l C q_k)$

With All Possible Pairs of j and l

Pushdown Automata → CFG

- Modification of Transition Functions

$\delta(q_0, a, z) = \{(q_0, Az)\}$
$\boxed{\delta(q_0, a, A) = \{(q_0, A)\}}$
$\delta(q_0, b, A) = \{(q_1, \lambda)\}$
$\delta(q_1, \lambda, z) = \{(q_2, \lambda)\}$

$\delta(q_0, a, A) = \{(q_3, \lambda)\}$
$\delta(q_3, \lambda, z) = \{(q_0, Az)\}$

⟹

$\delta(q_0, a, z) = \{(q_0, Az)\}$
$\delta(q_3, \lambda, z) = \{(q_0, Az)\}$
$\delta(q_0, a, A) = \{(q_3, \lambda)\}$
$\delta(q_0, b, A) = \{(q_1, \lambda)\}$
$\delta(q_1, \lambda, z) = \{(q_2, \lambda)\}$

Pushdown Automata → CFG

- Conversion into CFG

$\delta(q_0, a, z) = \{(q_0, Az)\}$
$\delta(q_3, \lambda, z) = \{(q_0, Az)\}$
$\delta(q_0, a, A) = \{(q_3, \lambda)\}$
$\delta(q_0, b, A) = \{(q_1, \lambda)\}$
$\delta(q_1, \lambda, z) = \{(q_2, \lambda)\}$

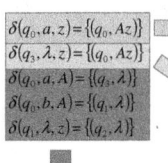

$(q_0 A q_3) \to a$
$(q_0 A q_1) \to b$
$(q_1 z q_2) \to \lambda$

$(q_0 z q_0) \to a(q_0 A q_0)(q_0 z q_0) \mid a(q_0 A q_1)(q_1 z q_0) \mid a(q_0 A q_2)(q_2 z q_0) \mid a(q_0 A q_3)(q_3 z q_0)$
$(q_0 z q_1) \to a(q_0 A q_0)(q_0 z q_1) \mid a(q_0 A q_1)(q_1 z q_1) \mid a(q_0 A q_2)(q_2 z q_1) \mid a(q_0 A q_3)(q_3 z q_1)$
$(q_0 z q_2) \to a(q_0 A q_0)(q_0 z q_2) \mid a(q_0 A q_1)(q_1 z q_2) \mid a(q_0 A q_2)(q_2 z q_2) \mid a(q_0 A q_3)(q_3 z q_2)$
$(q_0 z q_3) \to a(q_0 A q_0)(q_0 z q_3) \mid a(q_0 A q_1)(q_1 z q_3) \mid a(q_0 A q_2)(q_2 z q_3) \mid a(q_0 A q_3)(q_3 z q_3)$

$(q_3 z q_0) \to (q_0 A q_0)(q_0 z q_0) \mid (q_0 A q_1)(q_1 z q_0) \mid (q_0 A q_2)(q_2 z q_0) \mid (q_0 A q_3)(q_3 z q_0)$
$(q_3 z q_1) \to (q_0 A q_0)(q_0 z q_1) \mid (q_0 A q_1)(q_1 z q_1) \mid (q_0 A q_2)(q_2 z q_1) \mid (q_0 A q_3)(q_3 z q_1)$
$(q_3 z q_2) \to (q_0 A q_0)(q_0 z q_2) \mid (q_0 A q_1)(q_1 z q_2) \mid (q_0 A q_2)(q_2 z q_2) \mid (q_0 A q_3)(q_3 z q_2)$
$(q_3 z q_3) \to (q_0 A q_0)(q_0 z q_3) \mid (q_0 A q_1)(q_1 z q_3) \mid (q_0 A q_2)(q_2 z q_3) \mid (q_0 A q_3)(q_3 z q_3)$

Pushdown Automata → CFG

- Derivation of String

$(q_0, aab, z) \ (q_0, ab, Az) \ (q_3, b, z) \ (q_0, b, Az) \ (q_1, \lambda, z) \ (q_2, \lambda, \lambda)$

Derivation of aab by pushdown automata

$(q_0 z q_0) \Rightarrow a(q_0 A q_3)(q_3 z q_2) \Rightarrow aa(q_3 z q_2) \Rightarrow aa(q_0 A q_1)(q_1 A q_2) \Rightarrow aab(q_1 A q_2) \Rightarrow aab$

Derivation of aab by context free grammar

Summary and Exercises

- Summary

    Definition of Pushdown Automata
    $$M = (Q, \Sigma, \Gamma, \delta, q_0, z, F) \quad Q \times (\Sigma \cup \{\lambda\}) \times \Gamma \to Q \times \Gamma^*$$

    Acceptance of Language by the Pushdown Automata
    $$L(M) = \left\{ w \in \Sigma^* : (q_0, w, z) \vdash_M^* (q_f, \lambda, u), q_f \in F, u \in \Gamma^* \right\}$$

    Context Free Grammar → Pushdown Automata
    $$G = (V, T, S, P) \longrightarrow M = (\{q_0, q_1, q_f\}, T, V \cup \{z\}, \delta, q_0, z, \{q_f\})$$

    Pushdown Automata → Context Free Grammar
    $$(q_j, \lambda) \in \delta(q_i, a, A) \quad (q_i A q_j) \to a$$
    $$(q_k, BC) \in \delta(q_i, a, A) \quad (q_i A q_k) \to a(q_j B q_l)(q_l C q_k)$$
    With All Possible Pairs of j and l

Summary and Exercises

- Acceptance of String by PDA

$$M = (\{q_0, q_f\}, \{a,b\}, \{0,1,z\}, \delta, q_0, z, \{q_f\})$$

$\delta(q_0, \lambda, z) = \{(q_f, z)\}$

$\delta(q_0, a, z) = \{(q_0, 0z)\}$ aabb

$\delta(q_0, b, z) = \{(q_0, 1z)\}$ ababab

$\delta(q_0, a, 0) = \{(q_0, 00)\}$ aaaabbbabb

$\delta(q_0, b, 0) = \{(q_0, \lambda)\}$

$\delta(q_0, a, 1) = \{(q_0, \lambda)\}$

$\delta(q_0, b, 1) = \{(q_0, 11)\}$

Summary and Exercises

- Conversion into Greibach Normal Form

$$S \to CD, C \to c, D \to dc$$
$$S \to cdCD, C \to dc, D \to d$$
$$S \to aaAabB, A \to a, B \to baA$$
$$S \to AabBba, A \to aB, B \to b$$

Summary and Exercises

- CFG → PDA

$$S \to CD, C \to c, D \to dc$$
$$S \to cdCD, C \to dc, D \to d$$
$$S \to aaAabB, A \to a, B \to baA$$
$$S \to AabBba, A \to aB, B \to b$$

Summary and Exercises

- PDA → CFG

$\delta(q_0, a, A) = \{(q_0, \lambda)\}$ $\quad$ $\delta(q_0, a, A) = \{(q_0, BC)\}$
$\delta(q_0, b, A) = \{(q_1, \lambda)\}$ $\quad$ $\delta(q_0, b, A) = \{(q_1, \lambda)\}$
$\delta(q_1, \lambda, z) = \{(q_2, \lambda)\}$ $\quad$ $\delta(q_1, \lambda, z) = \{(q_2, \lambda)\}$

$\delta(q_0, a, A) = \{(q_0, A)\}$ $\quad$ $\delta(q_0, a, A) = \{(q_0, B)\}$
$\delta(q_0, b, A) = \{(q_1, \lambda)\}$ $\quad$ $\delta(q_0, b, A) = \{(q_1, \lambda)\}$
$\delta(q_1, \lambda, z) = \{(q_2, \lambda)\}$ $\quad$ $\delta(q_1, \lambda, z) = \{(q_2, \lambda)\}$

Context Free Languages Properties
Lecture 08

Outline

- Introduction
- Pumping Lemma
- Closure Properties
- Closure under Regular Intersection
- Summary and Exercises

Introduction

- Scope of this Lecture

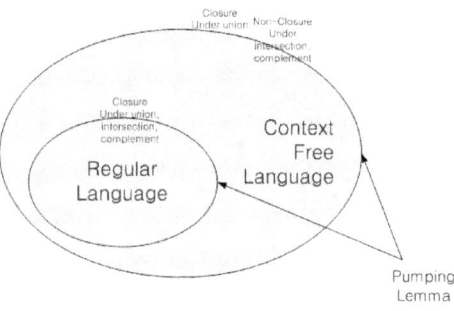

Introduction

- Review of Regular Languages
  - Definition of Regular Languages
    - Single Character or Empty String →Primitive One
    - r1 + r2, r1 r2, r1* → Regular Language
  - Representations of Regular Languages
    - Finite Automata
    - Regular Expression
    - Regular Grammar
  - Pumping Lemma $w = xyz \in L \rightarrow xy^i z \in L$
  - Closure under the following Operations
    - Set Operations: Union, Intersection, and Complement
    - String Operation: Concatenation and Star Closure

Introduction

- Review of Context Free Languages
    - Representations of Context Free Languages
        - Pushdown Automata
        - Context Free Grammar
    - Pumping Lemma:
    - Closure under Union, Catenation, and Star-Closure
    - Non-Closure under Intersection and Complementation

Introduction

- Regular Languages vs Context Free Languages

	Regular Language	Context Free Language
Automata	Finite Automata	Pushdown Automata
Input	Current State, Input Symbol	Current State, Input Symbol, Stack Symbol
Output	Next State	Next State, Stack String
Components	Input String, Control Unit	Input String, Control Unit, Stack

Introduction

- Goal of this Lecture
  - Identification of non Context Free Languages using Pumping Lemma
  - Realization of Existence of Linear Context Free Language as Proper Subset
  - Derivation of Context Free Grammar using Set Operations
  - Identification of non Context Free Languages using Closure under Regular Intersection

Pumping Lemma

- Definition of Pumping Lemma
  - but $|Q| \leq m$ → $|w| = \infty$ $|Q| << |w|$
  - Transition from a State into another by a Single Character
  - Repetition of States by Cycle as the Requirement for the String with
  - Repetition of Substrings as Components of a Long String

$$|w| = \infty$$

Pumping Lemma

- Pumping Lemma for Regular Languages

$$|Q| \leq m \quad |w| \geq m$$
$$w = xyz \quad |xy| \leq m \quad |y| \geq 1$$
$$\delta^*(q_0, x) = q_r \ \ \delta^*(q_r, y) = q_r \ \ \delta^*(q_r, z) = q_f$$
$$\delta^*(q_0, xz) = q_f, xz \in L \ \ \delta^*(q_0, xyz) = q_f, xyz \in L$$
$$\delta^*(q_r, xy^i z) = q_f, xy^i z \in L$$

Pumping Lemma

- Pumping Lemma for Context Free Languages

$$|Q| \le m \quad |w| \ge m$$
$$w = uvxyz \quad |vxy| \le m \quad |vy| \ge 1 \quad uv^i xy^i z \in L$$

Assumption: No Unit Production, No λ-Production, No Useless Production

Proof

$$S \stackrel{*}{\Rightarrow} uAz \stackrel{*}{\Rightarrow} uvAyz \stackrel{*}{\Rightarrow} uvxyz$$

$$A \stackrel{*}{\Rightarrow} vAy \quad A \stackrel{*}{\Rightarrow} x$$

$$uv^i xy^i z \in L$$

Pumping Lemma

- Proof of non Context Free Languages

$$L = \{a^n b^n c^n : n \geq 0\} \quad \text{Non Context Free Language}$$

$$vxy = a^k \implies uv^i xy^j z \notin L, \exists i \neq j$$

$$vxy = a^m b^m \implies vxy = a^{m-k} a^k b^m \quad |x| \geq 1$$

$$uv^i xy^j z \notin L, i \neq j$$

Pumping Lemma

- **Pumping Lemma for Linear Context Free Languages**

    If G is a linear context free grammar
    then L(G) is the linear context free language

    $L = \{a^n b^n : n \geq 0\}$ Linear Context Free Grammar

    $|Q| \leq m \quad |w| \geq m$

    $w = uvxyz \quad |uvxy| \leq m \quad |vy| \geq 1 \quad uv^i xy^i z \in L$

    $L = \{w : n_a(w) = n_b(w)\}$ Non Linear Context Free Grammar
    $w = a^m b^{2m} a^m \implies w = a^{m+k} b^{2m} a^{m+l}$
    u,v,y,z are a's

Closure Properties

- Overview of Closure Properties
    - Closure of Context Free Languages under Less Operations than Regular Languages
    - Closure of Context Free Languages under Union, Concatenation, and Star-Closure
    - Non-Closure of Context Free Languages under Intersection and Complement
    - Closure of Regular Languages under the All Five Operations

Closure Properties

- Closure under Union

$$G_1 = (V_1, T_1, S_1, P_1) \quad G_2 = (V_2, T_2, S_2, P_2)$$
$$V_1 \cap V_2 = \emptyset \quad \text{Assumption}$$
$$L(G_3) = L_1 \cup L_2$$
$$G_3 = (V_1 \cup V_2 \cup \{S_3\}, T_1 \cup T_2, S_3, P_3)$$
$$P_3 = P_1 \cup P_2 \cup \{S_3 \rightarrow S_1 \mid S_2\}$$
$$S_3 \Rightarrow S_1 \stackrel{*}{\Rightarrow} w \in L_1$$
$$S_3 \Rightarrow S_2 \stackrel{*}{\Rightarrow} w \in L_2$$

Closure Properties

- Closure under Concatenation

$$G_1 = (V_1, T_1, S_1, P_1) \quad G_2 = (V_2, T_2, S_2, P_2)$$
$$V_1 \cap V_2 = \emptyset \quad \text{Assumption}$$
$$L(G_4) = L_1 L_2$$
$$G_4 = (V_1 \cup V_2 \cup \{S_4\}, T_1 \cup T_2, S_4, P_4)$$
$$P_4 = P_1 \cup P_2 \cup \{S_4 \to S_1 S_2\}$$
$$S_4 \Rightarrow S_1 S_2 \stackrel{*}{\Rightarrow} w \in L_1 L_2$$

Closure Properties

- Closure under Star Closure

$$G_1 = (V_1, T_1, S_1, P_1)$$

$$L(G_5) = L_1^*$$
$$G_5 = (V_1 \cup \{S_5\}, T_1, S_5, P_5)$$
$$P_5 = P_1\{S_5 \to S_1 S_5 \mid \lambda\}$$
$$S_5 \Rightarrow S_1 S_5 \stackrel{*}{\Rightarrow} w \in L_1^*$$

Closure Properties

- Non Closure under Intersection

$L_1 = \{a^n b^n c^m : n \geq 0, m \geq 0\}$ $L_2 = \{a^n b^m c^m : n \geq 0, m \geq 0\}$

Context Free Language Context Free Language

$S \rightarrow S_1 S_2$
$S_1 \rightarrow a S_1 b \mid \lambda$
$S_2 \rightarrow c S_2 \mid \lambda$

$S \rightarrow S_1 S_2$
$S_1 \rightarrow a S_1 \mid \lambda$
$S_2 \rightarrow b S_2 c \mid \lambda$

$L_1 \cap L_2 = \{a^n b^n c^n : n \geq 0\}$

Closure under Regular Intersection

- Theorem

$L_1 \Longrightarrow$ Context Free Language $L_2 \Longrightarrow$ Regular Language

$$M_1 = (Q, \Sigma, \Gamma, \delta_1, q_0, z, F_1) \quad M_2 = (P, \Sigma, \delta_2, p_0, F_2)$$

$L_1 \cap L_2$ Context Free Language

$$\hat{M} = (\hat{Q}, \Sigma, \Gamma, \hat{\delta}, q_0, z, \hat{F}) \quad \begin{aligned} \hat{Q} &= Q \times P \\ \hat{q}_0 &= (q_0, p_0) \\ \hat{F} &= F_1 \times F_2 \end{aligned}$$

Closure under Regular Intersection

- Proof

$$M_1 = (Q, \Sigma, \Gamma, \delta_1, q_0, z, F_1) \qquad M_2 = (P, \Sigma, \delta_2, p_0, F_2)$$

$$(q_k, x) \in \delta_1(q_i, a, b) \qquad \delta_2(p_j, a) = p_l$$

$$((q_k, p_l), x) \in \hat{\delta}((q_i, p_j), a, b)$$

$$q_r \in F_1 \qquad\qquad\qquad\qquad\qquad p_s \in F_2$$

$$(q_0, w, z) \vdash^*_{M_1} (q_r, \lambda, x) \qquad \delta^*(p_0, w) = p_s$$

$$((q_0, p_0), w, z) \vdash^*_{\hat{M}} ((q_r, p_s), \lambda, x)$$

Closure under Regular Intersection

- Example of Proving Context Free Language

$L = \{a^n b^n : n \geq 0, n \neq 100\}$ Context Free Language

$L_1 = \{a^{100} b^{100}\}$ Regular Language

$\overline{L_1}$ Regular Language By Closure of Regular Language Under Complement

$L = \{a^n b^n : n \geq 0\} \cap \overline{L_1}$ Context Free Language
By Closure of Under Regular Intersection

Closure under Regular Intersection

- Example of Proving non Context Free Language

$$L = \{w \in \{a,b,c\}^* : n_a(w) = n_b(w) = n_c(w)\}$$
Non Context Free Language

$\{a^m b^n c^k : m \geq 0, n \geq 0, k \geq 0\}$ Regular Language

$L \cap \{a^m b^n c^k : m \geq 0, n \geq 0, k \geq 0\} = \{a^n b^n c^n : n \geq 0\}$
Non Context Free Language

Non Context Free Language
By Closure of Under Regular Intersection

Closure under Regular Intersection

- Decidability of Context Free Languages

S is a useless production after removing unit production, λ-Productions, and Useless Productions ⟹ $L(G) = \emptyset$

$A \overset{*}{\Rightarrow} xAy$ Repeating Variable

$S \overset{*}{\Rightarrow} uAz \overset{*}{\Rightarrow} uvAyz \overset{*}{\Rightarrow} uv^n xy^n z$ ⟹ $|L(G)| = \infty$

Summary and Exercises

- Summary
    - Regular Language vs Context Free Language
    - Pumping Lemma as the Tool for Identifying non Regular Language and non Context Free Language
    - Closure and Non Closure Properties of Context Free Languages
        - Closure Property: Union, Concatenation, and Star-Closure
        - Non Closure Property: Intersection and Complement
    - Closure Under Regular Intersection
        - Intersection of Context Free Language and Regular Language

Summary and Exercises

- Operations on Context Free Grammars

$S_1 \to AB$ $\qquad S_2 \to cdCD$
$A \to c$ $\qquad C \to dc$
$B \to dc$ $\qquad D \to d$

(1) Union
(2) Concatenation
(3) Star-Closure of Left
(4) Star-Closure of Right

Summary and Exercises

- Non Closure of Context Free Languages
  - Non Closure under Complement using
    $$L_1 \cap L_2 = (\overline{L_1} \cup \overline{L_2})^c$$
  - Non Closure under Difference using
    $$L_1 - L_2 = L_1 \cap \overline{L_2}$$
  - Non Closure under Symmetry Difference using $(L_1 \cap \overline{L_2}) \cup (\overline{L_1} \cap L_2)$
  - Non Closure under Symmetry Difference using $(L_1 \cup L_2) - (L_1 \cap L_2)$

Summary and Exercises

• Pushdown Automata by Regular Intersection

$M_1 = (\{q_0, q_f\}, \{a,b\}, \{0,1,z\}, \delta, q_0, z, \{q_f\})$

$\delta(q_0, \lambda, z) = \{(q_f, z)\}$
$\delta(q_0, a, z) = \{(q_0, 0z)\}$
$\delta(q_0, b, z) = \{(q_0, 1z)\}$
$\delta(q_0, a, 0) = \{(q_0, 00)\}$
$\delta(q_0, b, 0) = \{(q_0, \lambda)\}$
$\delta(q_0, a, 1) = \{(q_0, \lambda)\}$
$\delta(q_0, b, 1) = \{(q_0, 11)\}$

$M_2 = (\{q_0, q_1, q_2\}, \{a,b\}, \delta, q_0, \{q_2\})$

$\delta(q_0, a) = q_1, \delta(q_0, b) = q_2$
$\delta(q_1, a) = q_1, \delta(q_1, b) = q_1$
$\delta(q_2, a) = q_0, \delta(q_2, b) = q_2$

$L(\hat{M}) = L(M_1) \cap L(M_2)$

Derive the Pushdown Automata $\hat{M}$

Summary and Exercises

- Proof by Regular Intersection

$L_1 \Longrightarrow$ Context Free Language $\quad L_2 \Longrightarrow$ Regular Language

Prove the Closure under Regular Difference $\quad L_1 - L_2$

$L = \{a^n b^n : n \geq 0, n \neq 5\}$ Context Free Language

$L = \{a^n b^n : n \geq 1, n \% 2 = 1\}$ Context Free Language

$L = \{w \in \{a,b\}^* : n_a(w) = n_b(w)\}$ Context Free Language

www.ingramcontent.com/pod-product-compliance
Lightning Source LLC
Chambersburg PA
CBHW052148220526
45471CB00004B/1585